A SAMPLE MBA RESEARCH PROPOSAL FOR MBA

Preface

This ebook is a sample research proposal which the author did did when he was in Namibia in his Research Consultant.Students who are doing business courses like Tourism,business studies,administration , marketing and MBA are faced with the Research project in their final year and this proves to be very challenging.Sometimes they end up failing and fail to proceed to graduate.Therefore writer of this book has written this book to give a guideline on how to write a research proposal .The practical research is what most students need and this book can be used for literature review in your dissertation or thesis .It is a research done in Namibia in the tourism sector and most of the figures are accurate ,but the writer has left out the questionnaire and the bibliography.The reason is simple because this is not a guideline ,a sample research which you can modify to become yours in your chosen area of study.Therefore,its purpose is to help you write a research proposal that is sound for your degree specifically an MBA thesis.For a dissertation the format may slightly differ ,but overally this is a universally accepted format for any Research proposal

TOPIC: An evaluation of the economic development impact of tourism sector in job creation in Namibia

Name	**Mandisa Georgina**
Programme	**EMBA**
University	**University of Namibia**

This is in fulfillment of the Executive Masters for Business Administration Programme

List of abbreviations and terms

BEE	Black Entrepreneurship Empowerment
CBNRM	Community Based National Resources Management
CBT	Community Based Tourism
DEA	Directorate of Environmental Affairs
DPWM	Directorate of Parks and Wildlife Management
DRFN	Desert Research Foundation in Namibia
ECEAT	European Centre for Ecological and Agricultural Tourism
EU	European Union
FENATA	Federation of Namibian Tourism Associations
FIT	Frequent Individual Traveller
FTTSA	Fair Trade in Tourism South Africa
GRN	Government of Republic of Namibia
HDI	Historically Disadvantaged Individual
LIFE	Living in a Finite Environment
MET	Ministry of Environment and Tourism
MRLGH	Ministry of Regional and Local Government and Housinand Rural Development

NACOBTA	Namibia Community Based Tourism
Assistance Trust	
NACSO	Namibian Association of CBNRM
Support Organisations	

Executive summary

Tourism in Namibia is growing at a rate three times as fast as the world's average and has become the most important sector in the SADC region creating a lot of jobs. Tourism is the third largest contributor to Namibia's economy ("Travel and Tourism Economic Impact 2011: Namibia"). While the economic benefits are present, they are not evenly distributed among people in different areas and of different economic standing. The tourism industry is dominated by a few powerful corporations, most of which are based in the West. The consequences of a Westernized tourism industry are that the aspirations and needs of the developing countries receiving tourists are mostly neglected. Tourism has potential to be the source of greater economic benefits for the less developed countries in the world (Ardahaey 2011). The thesis will start with an introduction or preamble of the background of the impact studies and later gives an outline of the major methodological framework employed in Chapter1 .In chapter 2, the researcher will discuss the different literature, previous articles, journals of tourism, tourism board literature and the major keyword like economic development, tourism and the background of the tourism policy in the training of employees in Namibia. It will also look into how various boards view economic development .Chapter 3 will be focusing on the key word economic development from a regional, local and international perspective. It also discusses on the private sector contribution and lastly it discusses on the tourism potential of Namibia highlighting the major challenges in the economic policy implementation .Chapter 4 will discuss on the methodology used to survey the 50 key informants .It will highlights the case study, observation and the interview techniques used to make the interview and how each method will be used in the regions together with the sampling frame .It also will brings out the research instruments used and finally the ethical considerations in data collection in the research project .Chapter 5 is discussing on the data findings from the case study first ,interview and questionnaire key informants responses . The responses will be summarized and presented in Microsoft excel tables and SPSS package for data analysis. The analysis include four major areas of economic impact namely ,job creation, foreign exchange ,GDP and government fiscus contribution(taxes) .Chapter 6 is on conclusions and recommendations .The conclusion gives out the major findings in line with the objectives and addressing the research questions previous asked .Finally the recommendation are for other researchers to come , the government ,the key players in the tourism industry ant the major boards supervising tourism activities

1.0 Introduction

Tourism industry in Namibia

Since the dawn of mass tourism in the 60s the impacts of tourism have been more and more visible at tourist destinations. This implies also impacts other than the financial gains made by destinations, tour operators, national states, tourist entrepreneurs, and local residents. With an industry which is estimated to double from 2009 (880 million) until 2020 to 1.6 billion tourists ("Tourism 2020 Vision", 2010; "UNWTO World Tourism", 2010), it is most likely that tourism will make even larger footprints on our societies. Previous research on tourism impacts has predominantly focused on economic effects (Getz, 2009; Wall & Mathieson, 2006). However, it has been pointed out by several researchers that it is of importance to look beyond the economic impacts and include social, cultural, environmental and other impacts (Deery&Jago, 2010; Dogan, 1989; Gössling & Hall, 2008; Lankford & Howard, 1994; Pizam, 1978; Turner & Ash, 1975) together with economic impacts.

This thesis aims to contribute to the growing research focusing on more economic tourism impact evaluation also showing to lesser extend social, cultural and environmental impacts.

In the late 60s, fishing villages in southern Spain and on Spanish islands were, in a short period of time, transformed into cities to cater for the rising mass tourism invasion from northern Europe. The insufficient planning, the speculation over land, and the control over supply and demand by foreign tour operators, created negative impacts in the long-run for the destinations. The overdevelopment impacted negatively on the local environment and social fabric of the destination and as a result affecting the number of tourists and local residents' perception of tourism development negatively (Knowles & Curtis, 1999). The case of Mallorca can be seen as an example or a symbol for this development with negative impacts of mass tourism visible already 40 years ago (Lindström, 2003). The notion that large volumes of tourists concentrated to a limited destination (in size) could bring negative social and cultural impacts appears in research notes already in the 70s (Pizam, 1978; Turner & Ash, 1975).As a consequence, the research questions for this thesis will follow these discussions and are highlighted below:

1.2 Research questions

1 **What is the contribution of the tourism sector in Namibia in employment creation?**
2 **What impact in economic, social, cultural and environmental is tourism contributing?**

3 Who are the major employers in the tourism industry and why?

The first research question concerns the development of a framework that can be applied when the aim is to measure, describe and understand tourism impacts in an economic tourism development perspective, i.e. a methodological problem. The second research question concerns the empirical problem in a holistic approach and will use the economic framework developed in the first question to analyze and discuss the impacts due to the step in incremental tourism development. The result, having applied the framework, will also illustrate which stakeholders at the destination that experience negative impacts (costs) and which stakeholders that experience positive impacts (benefits), thus understanding not only the impact on the destination as a whole, but also the impact on the different stakeholder affected by tourism development at the destination.

1.3 Research objectives

The thesis would like to find out the following objectives

> *To find out the economic impact of tourism in the Namibian economy*
> *To compare the different impacts in the country in tourism sector*
> *To evaluate the different sectors offering employment in Namibia*

> *To identify opportunities for employment in tourism sector and the problems?*

1.4 Aims of the study

The thesis aims to develop a framework for evaluating tourism impacts from an economic perspective, or more specifically evaluating impacts on a destination facing increased demand through tourism development. The aim is also to measure, describe, and understand tourism impacts using empirical data from a case study and thereby contribute to the discussion on sustainable tourism development, both in an academic and in an industry context. The intention is to further more holistic methods in evaluating tourism impacts. The statistics found will also be compared in the economic, social, cultural and sustainable dimension and different sectors of the economy.

1.5. Scope of the study

The researcher is going to target the area Namibia in all tourism destinations including, hotels, lodges, rest camps, recreational sites (parks), and tourism bodies in the country ant the Ministry of tourism. The study unit will be a survey of the scope of the study can be shown below:

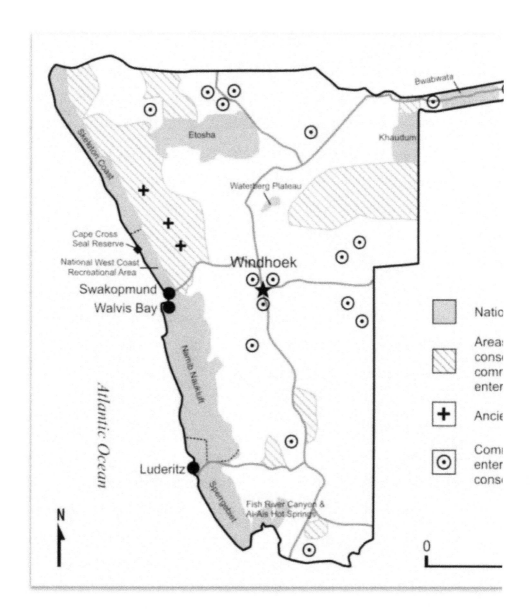

Fig 1 The map of Namibia Showing tourism destinations to be conducted research

1.6 Limitation of the study

The study looks too generalised in the whole Namibian circle and the tourism sector is not the significant sector in Namibia in employment generation. The area is too big for the researcher to finish it hence he has to use 4 main regions in proximity to her otherwise the cost would be insurmountable. There are very significant sectors such as mining and agriculture more than tourism in importance. The research is also purely economic hence limiting on other impacts in sustainable development, cultural, social and political. The researcher's main key informants will be those in the formal sector less tolerating the informal ones which holds a greater stake in the national cake proportion of tourism contribution. Although the research methodology is qualitative in nature most of the graphs a will be statistics in quantitative.

1.7 Significance of the study

Contribution of this thesis will hopefully be twofold. Firstly, it intends to contribute to the existing tourism research literature on the economic evaluation of tourism impacts from a broader, more holistic tourism development perspective. Moreover, it intends to add to the body of empirical knowledge, i.e. is tourism development at a rural or peripheral destination and urban platform , referring to the impacts found in relation to the step in incremental development, sustainable or not, why and to what degree? As a consequence the results will contribute to the discussion on the concept of economic tourism development. An empirical contribution will also hopefully be to see the results of a method, which has formerly not been frequently used, applied in a Namibian context. .The study will help the tourism players to improve their service delivery and encourage future students in the same topic to get a good foundation for literature review.

1.8 Chapter outline

The thesis has started with an introduction or preamble of the background of the impact studies and later gives an outline of the major methodological framework employed in Chapter1 .In chapter 2 the researcher will discuss the different literature, previous articles, journals of tourism, tourism board literature and the major keyword like economic development, tourism and the background of the tourism policy in the training of employees in Namibia. It will also look into how various boards view economic development .Chapter 3 is focusing on the key word economic development from a regional, local and international perspective. it also discusses on the private sector contribution and lastly it discusses on the tourism potential of Namibia highlighting the major challenges in the economic policy implementation .Chapter 4 discusses on the methodology used to survey the 50 key informants .It highlights the case study, observation and the interview techniques used to make the interview and how each method was used in the regions together with the sampling frame .It also brings out the research instruments used and finally the ethical considerations in data collection in the research project .Chapter 5 will discuss on the data findings from the case study first ,interview and questionnaire key informants responses . The responses are summarized and will be presented in Microsoft excel tables and SPSS package for data analysis. The analysis include four major areas of economic impact namely ,job creation, foreign exchange ,GDP and government fiscus contribution(

taxes)chapter 6 is on conclusions and recommendations .The conclusion gives out the major findings in line with the objectives and addressing the research questions previous asked .Finally the recommendation are for other researchers to come , the government ,the key players in the tourism industry ant the major boards supervising tourism activities .

1.9 Limitations of the study

Furthermore, given the time and financial limits on this study, it was necessary to limit both the types and number of enterprises. Similarly, the study will be limited to the four regions which will sampled by convenient sampling mentioned above even though there would have been other regions in Namibia worth including. The limited sample 0f 50 interviews pose an important challenge for generalization. However, the choice to include expert interviews provides a valuable tool for cross-checking the interview and observation material. In cases where the researcher was not sure about the validity of the informants' statements or my own observations, the expert interviews often provided supporting evidence. For example, the expert past interviews confirmed that several findings of this study are not restricted to the studied regions, but are in fact common throughout Namibia.

Chapter 2

2.0 LITERATURE REVIEW

2.1 Theoretical frame work

Over the past half century, tourism has evolved into one of the world's most powerful socio-economic forces, with 924 million international tourists in 2008 and an expected1.6 billion by 2020 (Telfer & Sharpley 2008: 1; UNWTO 2009). High growth rate in international tourism is closely related to increasing globalization, which has reduced the cost and time required to move commodities, services and people, and to increasing consumption by individuals in industrial, capitalist societies (Hall 2008: 36-49). Telferand Sharpley in their title *Tourism and development in the developing world* (2008) have introduced concept 'tourism–development dilemma', which refers to cases in which tourism is attractive as a means of stimulating social and economic development but where that development often fails to materialise or benefits only local elites and comes with significant costs to local communities. Similarly, Gössling et al. (2009: 113) remark that the benefit of tourism to society is highly complex and not self-evident.

However, before discussing the tourism–development dilemma more thoroughly it is important to define the concepts tourism and development. International tourism is a highly distinct economic sector comprising both production and consumption components and constituting a collection of industries that share similar functions and produce similar products (Cornelissen 2005b: 77). Sharpley(2002b: 23) lists a number of characteristics related to international tourism.

First of all, tourism is a leisure activity that is influenced by tourists' socio-cultural background, making it socially patterned. In addition, it is supported by a diverse, multi-sectored Industry and it is largely dependent upon the physical, social and cultural attributes of the destination. According to Sharpley (2009: 149), tourism is an inherent part of the processes of production and consumption aiming at economic profits inherent in modern capitalism.

2.1.2 Tourism defined

Tourism can be conceptualized as a global process of commodification and consumption involving flows of people, capital, images and cultures(Meethan 2001: 4).Tourism can be further described as an interdependent system that involves tourist generating and tourist receiving regions, between which lie transit regions through which the tourists travel . The fundamental characteristic of tourism is that the product is consumed in the receiving region, which is called the destination. A range of issues are prerequisites for tourism in the destination, while tourism is similarly influenced by a number of external factors in the tourist generating regions. According to Hall (2005b: 16-17), definitions of tourism tend to share common elements, including the temporary nature of travel by non-residents to destinations where they have a variety of impacts. In addition, tourism is primarily for leisure or recreation and involves voluntary movements of people. Finally, tourism may have an impact on, and influence the character of, a tourist. For this study, the definition of tourism by Dredge and

Jenkins (2007: 13) appears the most applicable. They defined tourism in the context of tourism policy as follows:

Tourism
- involves the movement of people and resources
- is characterized by a collection of government, businesses, activities and processes that
assist people in making decisions about travel
- involves the production and consumption of a range of tangible (e.g. tourism products)
and intangible (e.g. sense of place) resources
- overlaps and intersects with the daily lives of local communities
- involves the production and consumption of tourist experiences
- produces a range of intended and unintended consequences and effects that need to be
critically examined and managed

2.1.2 The term development explained

Development is similarly a multi-dimensional concept, which therefore embraces several definitions. It may be used as a philosophical concept and a guiding plan, while more broadly used it can refer to any progress implying some kind of positive transformation(Sharpley 2002b: 23). In this context, the concept is defined as it is used in social sciences and development studies. The term 'development', as it is currently used, dates from the post-war era of modern development thinking and is often used in Eurocentric manner to refer to a process of societies moving from one condition to another (Pieterse 2001: 5; Remeneyi 2004: 23). Koponen (2007: 50) points out that development can be viewed as a normative goal, as an actual social process and as unintentional intervention. He suggests that these dimensions can be studied as part of a

larger concept of 'developmentalism', which refers to the idea that development is good for all and it is in everybody's interests to promote it (Koponen 2009: 39). Furthermore, Olivier De Sardin (2005) has emphasized the need to pay attention to the various 'discourses of development' by different actors.

Sumner and Tribe (2008: 12-15) identify three different meanings within the concept of development. Development was defined as a long-term process of structural societal transformation, development as a short- to medium-term outcome of desirable targets, and development as a dominant discourse of Western modernity. In this study, all three dimensions can be regarded as valid and meaningful. In the Namibian context, the government in its national development policies, such as National Development Plans and Namibia Vision 2030, encompasses the notion of long-term process of structural transformation from a colonized, newly independent state to a politically and economically independent state with a high level of human welfare (National Planning Commission 2002; Republic of Namibia 2004, 2008). However, through the national development objectives Namibia also endorses medium-term desirable targets related to economy, society and the environment. On the other hand, the same objectives can be regarded as reflecting Western development discourse. For example, the national development objectives are safely anchored in the orthodox conceptualization of development predicated on ever-increasing economic growth and material accumulation.

Despite the relevance of such a practical definition, it is important to similarly include a more critical definition of development. Payne (2005) criticizes the underdevelopment-development dichotomy inherent in the development concept and argues that all countries in the world should pursue development. In his view, there are no explicitly developed or underdeveloped societies - instead, the current world and the status of different countries should be characterized as *unequal development*. Similarly,Swantz (2009), who is one of the pioneers in Finnish development studies, emphasizes the need to view development as a process that concerns all individuals, societies' andnations. Bond (2006: 11) applies the concept of *uneven development*, which implies that accumulation at one pole and poverty at another happen systematically, according to systems of exploitation.

The practical and critical definitions are equally important but may be applied in different contexts. Even though the researcher prefer to position herself among those who adopt a critical conceptualization of development and foresee that that there may be different paths of development, the researcher acknowledge that in a local context the practical definitions are more applicable. Furthermore, the concept of a 'developing country 'is applied in this study, despite its weakness and complexity. It refers to a loose group of countries in the southern hemisphere sharing similar characteristics in economic and human development, as well as similar geographical location and historical experience. Even though it is politically sensitive and difficult to define in exact terms, the researcher regard it as geographically more informative than more vague concepts of the 'Third World' and the 'Global South'. Furthermore, it is commonly used in the developmental settings and in the literature on development studies, even though it may not be fully applicable to Namibia, as it is to some other southern African countries.

2.2 Training in tourism sector

In-house training and competition for employees

Due to inadequate formal training opportunities in Namibia, it is common for privatetourism enterprises to train their own employees. For example, Wilderness Safaris, which has 13 lodges in Namibia, has trained thousands of tour guides and other personnel in the past 25 years in their own training programmer (Camp 2007). Nearly all the employees of the studied lodges and trophy hunting farms have been trained in the enterprises by the owners, managers or senior staff. However, some employees have been sent for short training courses provided by different institutions. In-house training can be viewed as entailing both opportunities and constraints. For local people in the Caprivi and Kavango regions there are hardly any other job opportunities available and furthermore, access to government posts is alleged to rely on existing personal and

political connections. In fact, unemployment in the Caprivi region is estimated at 80percent (Castro et al. 2007: 31). Therefore, access to tourism employment through in housetraining can be regarded as a significant opportunity.Even though the enterprises may provide sufficient skills for their employees, these rarely receive certificates of the acquired skills. Due to high costs of training by NATH and other NGOs, private employers may be reluctant to send their employees for recognized training courses. (Ash eke 2008). NAPHA courses for the employees of the trophy hunting farms are an exception as its members receive subsidized prices for the courses. Another problem is that in-house training often provides the employees only with the necessary skills for a certain field such as gardening, tracking animals, waitressing or cooking. Such concentration on specific narrow fields in training derives from the colonial times and may deny the employee the possibility to proceed to a higher level, which is at the core of transformation (Asheeke 2008). For example, an interviewed farm owner claims to have taught several of his employees how to drive but none of them has received an official driver's license, which would be a prerequisite for applying for a driver's position in tour operators.

According to a recent study by the Namibia Employers' Federation (Kadhikwa 2010), most private companies in Namibia perceive in-house training as ineffective. Although the studied enterprises did not complain about the effectiveness, the actual results indicate a need to improve formal training opportunities. In addition, the need for formal tourism training in the Caprivi and

Kavango regions was emphasised by the lodge informants.The constant demand for skilled people who can manage several tasks and possess sufficient language skills has led to private enterprises competing for employees by offering the potential recruit already working in another tourism enterprise a significantly higher salary and better career opportunities. This is referred to as 'poaching' andit similarly affects CBTEs, the employees of which are usually engaged in sponsored training in private training institutions. (Asheeke&Katjiuongua 2007: 59; Katjiuongua

2008; Siyambango 2009). The trained and most talented persons tend to be noticed and poached by the cooperating private enterprises. This implies a constant lack of trained

2.3 Inadequate experience and tourist gaze

Related to the lack of skills is the lack of experience in tourism. Even if a person is

trained with practical skills in one or several fields it does not necessarily mean that the

same person is familiar with the tourists' origin and the idea of hospitality (Asheeke&

Katjiuongua 2007: 60). This is where the white Namibians and well established private entrepreneurs are more advantaged, as pointed out by the owner of Livingstone Lodge:

Tourism planning and economic policy process in Namibia

According to Dredge and Jenkins (2007: 444), tourism planning is an activity that is concerned with identifying appropriate steps to achieve some predetermined goal and it occurs as a dialogue between overlapping or complementary and competing interests,communicative action, collaboration and capacity building. As Gunn with Var (2002)note, tourism planning involves various bodies such as private tourism companies,government, non-profit organizations and professional consultants, who all have their own interests and values. Hall (2008) presents different approaches to tourism planning which have been adopted from Getz (1987, in Hall 2008). Even though the approaches concern mainly developed countries, three of them apply to Namibian tourism planning, i.e. the economic tradition, community orientation and sustainable approach (Ministry of Environment and Tourism 2008; Republic of Namibia 2008; Becker 2009; Scholz 2009).

The economic tradition emphasises the role of tourism in creating economic growth,generating employment and enhancing regional development. Tourism is defined as an industry that has a measurable economic contribution and emphasis is placed on tourism marketing and promotion to attract those visitors who will be expected to provide the greatest economic benefit to the destination. Furthermore, economic goals are given priority over social and ecological aspects (Hall 2008: 56). According to Moscardo(2011), economic motives are at the core of tourism planning in most African countries, reflecting a hegemonic social representation of tourism planning. Such social representation is based on the assumption that tourism is necessary and desirable for a country and tourism is rarely evaluated against other development options (Moscardo2011: 433).

A sustainable approach to tourism planning is based on the concept of sustainable development. However, as Hall (2008: 62) states, the complex nature of the tourism industry and the often poorly defined linkages between its components are major barriers to the integrative strategic planning which is regarded as a prerequisite for sustainable development. In other words, a sustainable tourism industry requires a commitment by all parties involved in the planning process to sustainable development principles(Hall 2008: 67). Furthermore, according to Telfer and Sharpley (2008: 113), it is increasingly acknowledged that tourism cannot be planned in isolation, but needs to be integrated as part of broader development strategies within the context of sustainable development.The latter is particularly valid in southern Africa where tourism is expected to enhance broad-based development among the majority of the populations.

Only a year after independence, in 1991, the Namibian government declared tourism a priority sector, expected to diversify the economy. Since then, Namibian National Development Plans and government documents on tourism have acknowledged the role of tourism in promoting national development objectives

2.4 Tourism economic development as priority

The aridity of the country restricted the large scale development of agriculture and in addition, vast distances combined with a small population did not support small-scale manufacturing. (Jenkins 2000a: 114). At the same time, Namibia's natural and cultural assets provided a substantially good base for tourist attractions, which were scattered across the country and therefore could spread the development impact to those different areas. Furthermore, good roads and a generally sound infrastructure, together with safety, were useful assets for the evolving tourism industry. On the international tourism market, Namibia was perceived as a new and unexplored destination. Therefore, new tourism ventures and foreign investments in tourism started to flourish.(Roe et al. 2001).Namibia's Third National Development Plan (NDP3) set a target that by 2015there would be a National Tourism Master Plan in Namibia and that all regions, local authorities and conservancies would have tourism development plans by 2009 (Republic of Namibia 2008: 126). However, these targets proved to be overambitious, the slow process apparently being a product of the general lack of capacity and understanding of tourism in conservancies and local governments.

A major challenge for national and regional tourism planning is how to ensure a balance between the need for tourism growth and the need for tourism to contribute to local development needs. To achievethis balance cooperation is required from consultants who are commissioned to prepare the plans, and local stakeholders such as actors in the tourism sector and disadvantaged communities. Tourism planning is closely involved with tourism policy, which is inherently a government activity since governments decide what the policy objectives are and public policy is what governments decide to do (Colebatch 2002: 11). However, as the traditional roles of governments have been increasingly shifted to the private and volunteer sectors it has become difficult to define public policy as simply a government action(Dredge & Jenkins 2007: 10). On the other hand, the term 'public policy' specifically refers to government, whereas companies and organizations may have their own employment policies, environment policies, advertising policies etc. However, the role of government may differ across countries depending upon a range of variables, including a set of values governing policy approaches. In fact, Hall (2005a: 219) comments that there is increasing skepticism about the effectiveness of government and the intended consequences and impacts of government policy, including tourism policy.

2.5 Government policy towards economic development

It is important to acknowledge that different government policies and regulatory measures in other fields, such as the economy, conservation and the environment, affect the tourism policy and significantly influence the growth of tourism (Hall 2008:165). Furthermore, governments have many other roles in tourism in addition to policymaking, such as coordination, entrepreneurial activities, tourism promotion and protection of public interest (Hall 2008: 164-169). Scheyvens (2002) provides examples of some problems in government level tourism planning and policy making in developing countries. These include the top-down model of national planning and a lack of coordination from national to regional and local levels. In addition, within the government different ministries and departments dealing with issues related to tourism tend to be fragmented and fail to coordinate with each other.The Namibian tourism policy process started in 1995 and has involved more than 20 different workshops where the policy has been drafted and commented upon(Iihuhwa 2008). The first comprehensive draft was circulated for stakeholders in 2005and the second draft was completed in 2007. The final policy document, National Policy on Tourism for Namibia, was approved by the government on 4th December 2008and launched in June 2009 (Ministry of Environment and Tourism 2008). According to Wilkinson (1997), research on tourism policies, especially in developing countries, requires an understanding of national development policies. Namibia's tourism policy, as in the previous drafts, states that its aim is to provide a framework for the mobilization of tourism resources to realize the long term national goals of NDP3 (Ministry of Environment and Tourism 2008: 2). The vision of the policy is "a mature, sustainable and responsible tourism industry contributing significantly to the economic development of Namibia and the quality of life of all her people, primarily through job creation and economic growth" (Ministry of Environment and Tourism 2008: 2).

The policy has detailed sections on tourism infrastructure and investment, human resource development,marketing, planning and environmental sustainability. Notable improvements to the 2005 draft are sections which deal with tourism development on communal land and spreading the benefits of tourism to formerly disadvantaged Namibians, not only through community-based tourism but through a variety of measures. These include partnerships with the private sector, support for black economic empowerment, and codes of conduct for the investors and encouraging more women to become managers and owners of tourism enterprises. The Namibian government's market approach is reflected in the national tourism policy, which advocates a private sector and market driven approach to tourism. The role of the government is reduced to that of creating an enabling environment for the tourism industry and foreign investors. However, the Namibian government plays an active role within the tourism industry through government owned companies such as Air Namibia and Namibia Wildlife Resorts (NWR). Apart from economic benefits at a national level, the policy advocates local participation and a more equal spread of the benefits of tourism. The policy acknowledges that more Namibians should be provided with the skills to engage in tourism, including those at ownership and management

levels. Finally, the policy emphasises the need for environmental sustainability through environmental regulation and wildlife conservation. (Ministry of Environment and Tourism 2008). In other words,

3.0 METHODOLOGY
3.1 Data collection methods
3.1.1 Interviews

Qualitative interviewing begins with the assumption that the perspective of others is meaningful and knowable (Patton 2002: 341). The researcher conducted 28 interviews with 34 persons, some of who are couples (see detailed information in appendix). The researcher used an interview guide which is a thematic list of the questions or issues that are to be explored in the course of an interview. In my case, the interview guide included the six tourism economic and employment objectives of which the researcher wanted to hear the informants' perceptions and experiences. The guide makes interviewing a number of different people more systematic and comprehensive by delimiting in advance the issues to be explored. However,the interviewer has to remain flexible to establish a conversational atmosphere and to pursue the detail that is salient to each individual participant (Patton 2002: 343; Ritchie and Lewis (2003: 115). Hirsjärvi and Hurme (2000: 48) refer to the use of an interview guide as 'focused interview' and regard it as useful in stressing the importance of the interviewees' own interpretation of and meaning attached to the topics

3.1.2 Observation

Observation is an essential method in qualitative studies and it can occur at different levels (Patton 2002; Flick 2006). Eskola and Suoranta (2005) distinguish between participant observation and other observation according to the role of the researcher. The role in the tourism enterprises seemed to vary between that of a paying customer, a university student/researcher and a curious outsider who was soon regarded more or less as a friend. Hirsjärvi et al. (1997) and Tuomi and Sarajärvi (2002) remind us that while it is possible to distinguish the two extremes of systematic, outsider observation and reflexive participatory observation, only rarely does the actual observation technique represent either of these extremes, instead usually falling somewhere in between.The researcher used observation as an additional method in all the tourism enterprises except for two tour operators . The observations were documented in field notes and a research diary which were compiled on a daily basis throughout both field periods. Unfortunately the language barrier to some extent reduced my possibilities to observe the enterprises. For example, in two trophy hunting farms the owners and theiremployees communicated only in Afrikaans, whereas the employees used their vernacular-languages amongst themselves. Similarly, in CBTEs the people speak their local-languages, which made observation more difficult.The purpose of the observation was to deepen my understanding of the issues raised in the interviews and to acquire a more complete picture of the enterprises.

This proved valuable as observation revealed aspects which could not be drawn from the interviews. These include the power relations between employers and employees in the enterprises, values and attitudes, various challenges in the community-based enterprise and different socio-cultural contexts of the informants. Furthermore, there were several-issues brought up in the interviews that I wanted to counter-check through observation. Similarly, observation provided me with a broader and deeper picture of the entire-tourism–development nexus in Namibia. Time constraints limited my possibility too bserve everything I wanted and therefore I had to limit myself to issues that were of most importance. As Vilkka (2006: 13, 35) remarks, scientific observation is always selective and observation can elicit tacit knowledge from the informants, which can-diversify the material gathered through interviews.

3.1.2 Case study

Apart from academic literature, various policy documents, case studies and research reports of different Namibian tourism institutions have been valuable sources of information. I started by looking for relevant documents and reports by the Namibian government, such as the draft tourism policy, other tourism related policies, national development plans, and Vision 2030 and MET discussion papers on tourism. Soon it became clear that there are a number of non-governmental institutions in Namibia which produce similarly important reports on the specific topics that I am interested in.These include the Namibia Community Based Tourism Assistance Trust, the Namibian Association of CBNRM Support Organisations, the Institute for Public Policy Research and the Labour Resource and Research Institute. At the international scale, the documents by the World Tourism Organisation and the World Travel and Tourism

Council have provided statistics on the scope of tourism worldwide and in southern Africa. In addition, reports by the Overseas Development Institute cover a wide range of topics related to tourism and poverty reduction. Furthermore, several historical novels, autobiographies and other non-academic writings have deeply enhanced my knowledge and understanding of Namibian and southern African history and development, the legacy of apartheid and the interface of colonialism and nature conservation throughout Africa. Those authors specifically worth mentioning include Namhila (2001), Khaxas (2005), Leys and Brown (2005), Kekäläinen (2006), Kaakunga (2007), Maathai (2007, 2009) and Löytty (2008).

3.1.3 Questionnaire.

The aim of the questionnaire is to gather information specific information about a particular subject of research. The researcher ensured that the information to be gathered will have some tolerable accuracy and completeness. The layout of the questionnaire was kept very simple to encourage meaningful participation by the respondents. The questions were kept as concise as possible with care taken to the actual wording and phrasing of the questions. The reason being that the appearance and layout of the questionnaire are of great importance in any survey where the questionnaire is to be completed by the respondent (Loubser, 1999:287). The literature in the study was used as guidelines for the development of the questions in the questionnaire. The questions that were used in the questionnaire are:

- Dichotomous questions;
- Multiple-choice questions; and
- Five-point Likert scale type questions.

A dichotomous question is a question which offers two alternative answers to choose from. A multiple-choice question is a fixed question with more than two alternative answers, whilst a Likert scale is a verbal scale which requires a respondent to indicate a degree of agreement or disagreement. The combination of the three types of questions ensures the collection of complete information from the respondents (Loubser, 1999:221).Dichotomous questions were used because of the following reasons (Cooper & Schindler, 2003:377):

- Some questions in the questionnaire have only two possible answers. For example, questions relating to the gender of the respondents; and
- The ease of coding and analyzing, since the responses are predetermined. Multiple-choice questions were used for the study because of the following reasons

(Cooper & Schindler, 2003:377-379):

- These types of questions are easy to answer by the respondents. Non-response error is

thereby reduced; and

- The ease of coding and analyzing since the responses are predetermined.

Five-point Likert scale questions were used by the researcher for the following reasons
(Cant, 2003:113):

- It eliminates the development of response bias amongst the respondents;
- It assesses attitudes, beliefs, opinions and perception;
- Using a Likert scale makes the response items standard and comparable amongst the

Respondents; and

- Responses from the Likert scale questions are easy to code and analyse directly from

the questionnaires.

3.1.4. Questionnaire Items

A questionnaire containing 30 questions was utilized. The questionnaires were emailed to the target population that live across the divide of Namibia and some were filled whilst the researcher was waiting in some lodges where ample time was enough to some key informants however questionnaire were delivered face-face to those in the vicinity of Oshawa region tourism operators being the town in which the researcher reside. In the event if the return rate which was poor, the researcher conducted telephonic interviews with 10 additional respondents. The questions were framed to answer the research questions, as well as to test issues raised in the literature review. The questionnaire will comprised of closed ended questions. A 5-point Likert scale will be used. The Likert scale is a widely used means for measuring attitudes. Respondents indicate their own attitudes by stating how strongly they agree or disagree with statements. The primary method of collecting the questionnaires was by e-mail.

3.3 Pre-testing (pilot survey)

Pre-testing refers to the testing of the questionnaire on a small sample of respondents to identify and eliminate potential questions. All the aspects of the questionnaire should be tested, including wording sequence and layout. The respondents in the pre-test should be similar to those who will be included in the actual survey (Roberts-Lombard, 2002:132).Pre-testing is critical for identifying questionnaire problems. These can occur for both respondents and interviewers regarding question content, "skip patterns," or formatting. Problems with question content include confusion with the overall meaning of the question, as well as misinterpretation of individual terms or concepts. Problems with how to skip or navigate from question to question may result in missing data and frustration for both interviewers and respondents. Questionnaire formatting concerns are particularly relevant to self-administered questionnaires, and if unaddressed may lead to the loss of vital information (Snijkers, 2002:97).

The questionnaire was pre-tested in a pilot study involving 10 tourism operators where the researcher resides is near in Oshakati . A pilot study is described as the using of a questionnaire on a trial basis. Pre-testing is essential if the researcher is satisfied that the questionnaire being developed will perform its various functions in the interview situation. Furthermore, the data collected will be relevant and as accurate as possible, the target respondents will participate and co-operate as fully as possible and the collection and analysis of data will proceed smoothly (Cooper & Schindler, 2003:320). Pre-testing was used in the study to identify flaws in the questionnaire and to determine the time required by a respondent to complete the questionnaire. Furthermore, in the study at hand pre-testing the questionnaire was to test its face and content validity, and to identify and rectify problem areas. After pre-testing the instrument, it was refined for the data to be collected. The pre-test reviewed that some of the respondents were not willing to divulge their age and educational levels. The respondents did not understand some of the concepts and questions in the questionnaire and this resulted in the researcher coming up with an explanatory note to some questions. Furthermore, the arrangements of some of the questions were faulty. The result of the pre-test, consequently, led to some amendments to the questionnaire. The researcher was able to obtain most of the required information

3.4 Ethical issues

My aim has been to handle and present the research material in an ethical manner. This includes informed consent, anonymity and confidentiality, which are generally perceived-as important tenets of scientific research (Denscombe 2002; Scheyvens&Storey2003). Furthermore, Scheyvens and Storey (2003: 140) remark that any research process must ensure the participants' dignity and safety. When the researcher first approached the enterprises in Namibia, the researcher explained the purpose of her study and asked their permission to include them. In addition, before each interview and use of the digital recorder she re-introduced herself and the purpose of the study to the particular informant to ensure his or her willingness to participate in the research. All the enterprises and informants except the interviewed experts were guaranteed anonymity and therefore the researcher refers to the enterprises with pseudonyms. Some of them may be identifiable by those who are familiar with the local context, but in sensitive statements the researcher have protected both individual and enterprise anonymity so that they cannot be identified. However, the researcher decided to keep more critical comments to herself and discuss them through her publications.